Donald Trump's Wackiest Quotes

& other crazy stuff

Carter Hayes

CARTERHAYES

First published in Great Britain in 2024
Copyright © Michael Kempster Publishing 2024

Introduction

To some Donald Trump is a business magnate and a reality television star. To others he's a politician, even a political trailblazer. To many though he's a lightning rod for controversy, a symbol of brashness and excess, and a man whose every move elicits strong reactions, both good and bad. Love him or hate him, Donald J. Trump has undeniably left an indelible mark on the fabric of American society and is likely to do so well in to the future.

Born on June 14, 1946, in Queens, New York City as one of four children, Trump was raised in a family of real estate developers. From an early age, he showed a knack for business and a relentless drive to succeed. After graduating from the Wharton School at the University of Pennsylvania, Trump joined the family business, eventually taking the reins and building a vast empire of hotels, casinos, and skyscrapers.

Notwithstanding his success as a developer, it was Trump's foray into the world of reality television that catapulted him into the national spotlight. As the host of "The Apprentice," Trump became a household name, thanks in part to his catchphrase, "You're fired!" His larger-than-life persona and no-nonsense approach endeared him to millions of viewers, solidifying his status as a popular icon.

In 2016, Trump shocked the world by entering the race for the presidency as a Republican candidate. Despite facing scepticism from the political establishment and the media, Trump's unconventional campaign struck a chord with voters disillusioned by the status quo. In a stunning upset, he defeated Democratic nominee Hillary Clinton to become the 45th President of the United States.

Throughout his presidency, Trump continued to defy expectations, reshaping the political landscape with his unapologetic style and populist rhetoric. From contentious policy decisions to headline-grabbing Twitter feuds, Trump's tenure in the Oval Office was marked by controversy, chaos, and unprecedented levels of media scrutiny.

As his presidency came to a close, Trump left behind a legacy that remains deeply polarizing. To some, he's a champion of American values, a disruptor who challenged the political establishment and fought tirelessly for his vision of a "Make America Great Again." To others, he's a rabble-rouser, a threat to democracy, and a symbol of division and disorder.

Love him or loathe him, one thing is certain: Donald Trump is a figure unlike any other in American history. His words, actions, and larger-than-life persona have left an indelible imprint on the collective consciousness of the nation. And in "Donald Trump's Wackiest Quotes," we invite you to explore the lighter side of this complex and enigmatic figure, one outrageous quote at a time. Each quote interspersed with little known facts about the man himself and anecdotes from his colourful life.

"My fingers are long and beautiful, as, it has been well documented, are various other parts of my body."

March 30, 2011.

Audience: Response to a Vanity Fair article.
Context: Trump's defence against a journalist's critique included boasting about his physical appearance, a move characteristic of his confrontational and unorthodox style.

The Skating Rink Savior

In the mid-1980s, New York City struggled for years with the renovation of the Central Park Wollman Skating Rink. With costs soaring and progress stalling, Trump stepped in, offering to take over the project. He managed to complete the rink renovation in just three months, under budget and ahead of schedule. This accomplishment was widely publicized and served as a testament to Trump's efficiency and capability to get things done. It not only earned him praise from grateful New Yorkers but also bolstered his public image as a can-do businessman, an image that he would leverage in his future political career.

"I will build a great wall – and nobody builds walls better than me, believe me – and I'll build them very inexpensively.

June 16, 2015.

Audience: Supporters at his Presidential campaign announcement.
Context: Trump used this promise to emphasize his focus on immigration reform and border security which became a cornerstone of his 2016 campaign.

WWE Hall of Famer: Trump has a unique connection to the world of professional wrestling. He has appeared at several Wrestle Mania events and was inducted into the WWE Hall of Fame in 2013 in the celebrity wing.

"I could stand in the middle of Fifth Avenue and shoot somebody, and I wouldn't lose any voters, okay? It's like incredible."

January 23, 2016.

Audience: Campaign rally in Iowa.
Context: Trump's remark about his supporters' loyalty was seen as an extreme expression of confidence in his political base.

Boarding Air Force One with Toilet Paper on His Shoe

In a moment that became fodder for late-night television and social media memes, Trump was seen boarding Air Force One with what appeared to be a piece of toilet paper stuck to his shoe. The incident was harmless but it underscored how every moment of a President's life is scrutinized and how minor embarrassments can become global news.

"When Mexico sends its people, they're not sending their best. [...] They're sending people that have lots of problems, and they're bringing those problems with us. They're bringing drugs. They're bringing crime. They're rapists. And some, I assume, are good people."

June 16, 2015.

Audience: Supporters at his presidential campaign announcement.

Context: This controversial statement was part of Trump's broader discussion on immigration, which became a highly debated topic throughout his campaign and presidency.

Teetotaller: Despite owning wineries and being involved in various businesses that sell alcohol, Donald Trump abstains from drinking alcohol. This personal choice is partly attributed to the tragic death of his brother Fred Trump Jr., who struggled with alcoholism.

"You know, it really doesn't matter what the media write as long as you've got a young, and beautiful, piece of ass."

Unknown date – 1991

Audience: Interview with Esquire magazine.

Context: Trump's comment reflected his views on media attention and celebrity status, showcasing his often provocative approach to public statements.

The Unexpected Pizza Fork Incident

In 2011, during a visit to a pizza restaurant in New York with Sarah Palin, Trump was photographed eating a slice of pizza with a knife and fork. This unusual method sparked a media frenzy and public debate because for most people eating pizza with their hands is considered the norm, especially in New York City. Trump defended his choice by saying it was a more elegant way to eat pizza, especially the crust-heavy first bite. This incident highlighted Trump's knack for staying in the public eye, sometimes through unconventional means, and his ability to turn even something a simple as eating a slice of pizza into headline news.

"The beauty of me is that I'm very rich."

March 17, 2011.

Audience: ABC News interview.

Context: Trump was discussing his potential as a presidential candidate, highlighting his wealth as an advantage in political campaigning where the price tag to even get nominated can run in to many millions.

Education: Donald Trump graduated from the Wharton School of the University of Pennsylvania in 1968 with a degree in economics, and he often cites his attendance at Wharton as evidence of his intelligence.

"My IQ is one of the highest — and you all know it! Please don't feel so stupid or insecure; it's not your fault."

May 8, 2013.

Audience: Twitter.

Context: Known for continually boasting about his accomplishments and abilities, Trump made this statement on social media, which was in line with his self-promotion campaign.

The Trump Steaks Venture

Among the myriad of Trump-branded products, Trump Steaks is perhaps one of the most curious. Launched in 2007, these steaks were sold exclusively through The Sharper Image stores, an odd choice given the retailer's focus on electronics and gadgets. The venture was short-lived, with reports of poor sales leading to discontinuation of sales. Trump Steaks are another classic example of his strategy of extending the Trump Brand to a wide array of products, not all of which meet with success.

"Despite the constant negative press covfefe"

May 31, 2017.

Audience: Twitter.
Context: This incomplete tweet became famous for its mysterious ending, sparking widespread speculation and humour. It showcased Trump's often unfiltered use of social media. Written late at night it was very likely that he was nodding off as he typed the Tweet.

Historic Win: Donald Trump was the first U.S. president with no prior military or government service experience to hold office as President. More incredulously he actually won the presidency in 2016 as a Republican candidate, despite having been a registered Democrat until 2009.

"Nobody knew health care could be so complicated."

February 27, 2017.

Audience: Meeting with the National Governors Association.

Context: This comment was made in the context of his efforts to repeal and replace the Affordable Care Act, illustrating Trump's underestimation of the complexity of healthcare policy.

The Secret Chinese Bank Account

During Trump's presidency, it was revealed that he maintained a bank account in China, raising questions about his financial entanglements with foreign countries. This revelation was particularly striking given his tough stance on China and claims of bringing jobs back to America. The account highlighted the complex web of international business dealings that Trump was engaged in and the potential conflicts of interest that could potentially arise from a President with such a broad global business footprint.

--

Ancestral Roots: Trump's mother, Mary Anne MacLeod, was born in Scotland and emigrated to the United States in 1930. His father, Fred Trump, was a second-generation German-American. Donald Trump has expressed pride in his Scottish and German heritage.

"We're going to win so much, you're going to be so sick and tired of winning."

May 2016.

Audience: Campaign rally.

Context: Trump used this phrase repeatedly to promise success in various domains, from economic growth to international relations during his presidency.

Board Game: In 1989, Trump ventured into the board game market with a game called "Trump: The Game," which was a Monopoly-esque game where players could buy and sell real estate. The game was not a huge success and is now a collectors' item.

Promoting Hydroxychloroquine

Throughout the COVID-19 pandemic, Trump was a vocal advocate for the use of hydroxychloroquine as a treatment, despite a lack of scientific evidence supporting its effectiveness against the virus at the time. His promotion of the drug led to a surge in demand and a polarized response from the medical community and the public. This situation underscored the influence of presidential endorsement on public health practices and more worryingly the dangers of promoting unproven treatments.

"China is not our friend."

Various occasions.

Audience: General public, through various platforms including social media.
Context: Reflecting Trump's stance on China, emphasizing trade imbalances and economic competition as central issues in his foreign policy.

Space Force: Trump was responsible for the creation of the United States Space Force, the sixth branch of the U.S. Armed Forces and the first new military service since the Air Force was created in 1947. The Space Force was established in December 2019.

"What you're seeing and what you're reading is not what's happening."

July 24, 2018.

Audience: Veterans of Foreign Wars convention.
Context: Trump's critique of the media and its coverage of his administration, suggesting that reporting was not reflective of reality.

We're Going to Mars Very Soon

Trump's enthusiasm for space exploration was evident when he directed NASA to accelerate its plans for a manned mission to Mars, stating that it could happen "very soon." While ambitious, this statement oversimplified the enormous technical, financial, and temporal challenges associated with such a mission. It showcased Trump's preference for bold declarations that often outpaced current capabilities and plans.

"I've never seen a thin person drinking Diet Coke."

October 14, 2012.

Audience: Twitter.
Context: One of Trump's many personal observations shared on social media, showcasing his penchant for making broad, often humorous generalizations.

Financial Disclosures: Donald Trump broke with decades of presidential tradition by refusing to release his tax returns, citing ongoing audits. This decision sparked widespread speculation and legal battles over the details of his wealth and financial dealings.

"Why do we want all these people from 'shithole countries' coming here?"

January 11, 2018.

Audience: Oval Office meeting with lawmakers on immigration.
Context: Trump's remark during a discussion on protections for immigrants from Haiti, El Salvador, and African countries, which was met with accusations of racism and sparked international outrage.

The Inauguration Crowd Size Claim

One of the first controversies of Trump's presidency revolved around the size of his inauguration crowd. Despite photographic evidence to the contrary, Trump and his administration insisted that his inauguration had drawn the largest audience ever. This claim led to widespread discussions about "alternative facts," a phrase coined by Counselor to the President Kellyanne Conway when defending the administration's position. The incident set the tone for a presidency that would frequently clash with the media and facts regarding crowd sizes and other events.

"I am the chosen one."

August 21, 2019.

Audience: Speaking to reporters.
Context: Made while discussing the trade war with China, Trump looked up to the sky as he said this, leading to interpretations that he saw himself as delivered from a divine being and uniquely positioned to tackle difficult issues.

Personal Authorship: Trump has authored more than a dozen books, with "The Art of the Deal" (1987) being the most famous. In this book, he outlines his perspective on business and negotiation, and it became a bestseller, contributing significantly to his public persona as a successful businessman.

"When you're a star, they let you do it. You can do anything."

2005, revealed in October 2016.

Audience: "Access Hollywood" recording.
Context: This comment was made in a private conversation with Billy Bush, caught on a hot mic. It sparked a major controversy during the 2016 presidential campaign, highlighting issues of consent and misogyny.

Reviving "Merry Christmas"

Trump often claimed credit for bringing back the phrase "Merry Christmas," asserting that Americans were saying it more frequently because of his presidency. He positioned this as part of his campaign against what he perceived as political correctness gone too far, appealing to his base with the promise to uphold traditional values. While the claim was more symbolic than factual, it resonated with many who felt cultural and religious expressions were being marginalized. Again this showcased Trump's knack for tapping into cultural grievances as a source of political support.

"Windmills are tremendous. If you're into this. Tremendous."

Various, including during presidency.

Audience: Public speeches and social media.
Context: Trump's comments on wind energy often included critiques about their aesthetics, noise, and supposed dangers to birds, reflecting his scepticism of renewable energy sources.

Beauty Pageant Ownership: Trump owned the Miss Universe, Miss USA, and Miss Teen USA beauty pageants from 1996 until 2015. His involvement brought both increased publicity and controversy to the pageants.

"I have a great relationship with the blacks. I've always had a great relationship with the blacks."

April 14, 2011.

Audience: Talk1300 radio interview.
Context: Trump's attempt to appeal to African American voters was widely criticized for its awkward phrasing and numerous generalizations.

The Birth Certificate Controversy

Long before his presidential campaign, Donald Trump was a leading figure in the "Birther" movement, which falsely claimed that President Barack Obama was not born in the United States and therefore ineligible to be President. Trump's repeated calls for Obama to release his birth certificate to prove his citizenship gained significant media attention, culminating in Obama releasing his long-form birth certificate in 2011. This episode showcased Trump's knack for leveraging controversy and media coverage to remain in the public eye, a tactic that he would employ throughout his political career. The birther controversy also highlighted Trump's willingness to engage in divisive politics, setting the stage for his polarizing presidential campaign.

"I think, therefore I am. I tweet, therefore I am Donald Trump."

Various occasions.

Audience: General public, via social media and interviews.

Context: Trump has often emphasized the importance of Twitter as a direct communication tool with the public, bypassing traditional media.

Trump Ice Bottled Water: Trump ventured into the bottled water market in 2004 with Trump Ice. Marketed as "pure natural spring water," it was sold primarily at Trump properties and selected retailers. The brand was discontinued in 2010.

The Gold-Plated Helicopter

Trump's fondness for opulence is perhaps nowhere more evident than in his personal transportation, including a Sikorsky S-76 helicopter, lavishly outfitted with 24-karat gold-plated fixtures. This helicopter, often used to shuttle between his various properties or for high-profile entrances, is emblematic of his luxurious lifestyle and love for extravagance. The gold-plated helicopter not only served a practical purpose but also acted as a flying symbol of his wealth and status, reinforcing his image as a successful and flamboyant businessman.

"Space Force, because it's a whole... we need it, we need it."

March 13, 2018

Audience: Military personnel.

Context: Trump announced his intent to create a new branch of the U.S. military focused on space, emphasizing national security concerns and technological advancements during a speech at Marine Corps Air Station Miramar.

The Solar Eclipse Moment

In August 2017, during a solar eclipse, Trump momentarily looked directly at the sun without protective eye wear, contrary to widespread safety advisories. This brief act, captured during a viewing event at the White House, became an instantly memorable image, generating a mix of humor and disbelief on social media and in the news. It underscored Trump's tendency to defy conventions and expert advice, even in trivial matters, contributing to his nonconformist image.

"The concept of global warming was created by and for the Chinese in order to make U.S. manufacturing non-competitive."

November 6, 2012 (Twitter).

Audience: General public.

Context: Trump has been critical of climate change science, and this tweet reflected his conspiracy theory about China both driving the global warming narrative and benefiting from it.

Missed the 1968 Draft: Despite being eligible for the military draft during the Vietnam War, Trump received four student deferments while attending college and one medical deferment for bone spurs in his heels, which he has since said were "temporary."

"I have a great relationship with the Mexican people."

Multiple occasions.

Audience: Various, including interviews and speeches.
Context: Despite his tough stance on immigration and border security, Trump has claimed to maintain positive relations with Mexican nationals.

Person, Woman, Man, Camera, TV

In an interview, Trump described taking a cognitive test and made a point of recalling the words "person, woman, man, camera, TV" in order—a sequence he repeated to emphasize his mental acuity. The moment went viral, spawning memes and discussions about the nature of cognitive testing and the President's fitness for office. It highlighted Trump's high sensitivity to questions about his competence and his unique, albeit often misguided, approach to countering criticism.

"Bad hombres."

October 19, 2016 (Third presidential debate).

Audience: National television audience.

Context: Discussing immigration and border security, Trump used this phrase to refer to criminal elements coming into the U.S. from Mexico, which drew attention for its colloquialism.

Hosted "Saturday Night Live": Trump hosted the popular television show "Saturday Night Live" twice, first in 2004 and again in 2015 during his presidential campaign. His appearances generated both praise and criticism.

The Trump Board Game

In 1989, Donald Trump ventured into the board game industry with "Trump: The Game." The game, which bore the tag line "It's not whether you win or lose, but whether you win!" was reminiscent of Monopoly but centered around Trump's real estate ventures. Players could engage in buying, selling, and trading properties, aiming to amass a fortune large enough to rival Trump's own. Despite the initial hype, the game did not perform well in sales. This foray into gaming again shows Trump's constant search for branding opportunities, a trait that he carried into his presidential campaign.

"We have the best military, but we don't win any more... We can't beat ISIS. Give me a break."

February 19, 2016

Audience: Campaign rally attendees.

Context: Critiquing the Obama administration's foreign policy during a campaign rally in Myrtle Beach, SC, Trump emphasized his belief that the U.S. was under performing on the global stage, particularly against ISIS.

"We won with poorly educated. I love the poorly educated."

February 24, 2016

Audience: Supporters.

Context: Celebrating his electoral successes at the Nevada caucus, Trump famously tried to show how he appreciated the support from voters across all educational backgrounds but again this quote is singled out for its unusual phrasing.

The Hollywood Walk of Fame Star

Donald Trump's star on the Hollywood Walk of Fame, awarded in 2007 for his work as producer and host of "The Apprentice," has been a recurring target for vandalism since he announced his presidential bid. The star has been defaced with paint, marked with swastikas, and even destroyed with a pickaxe on multiple occasions. Each incident of vandalism sparks a wave of media coverage.

Nominated for Nobel Peace Prize: Trump was nominated for the Nobel Peace Prize in 2021 for his administration's efforts to broker peace agreements between Israel and several Arab countries, including the Abraham Accords.

"Russia, if you're listening, I hope you're able to find the 30,000 emails that are missing."

July 27, 2016 (Press conference).

Audience: National television audience.

Context: In the midst of the 2016 election, Trump's comment was seen as encouraging foreign intervention in American politics, sparking significant controversy.

The Trump Taj Mahal

One of Trump's most ambitious projects was the Trump Taj Mahal in Atlantic City, which opened in 1990. Billed as the world's largest and most opulent casino, Trump claimed it would be the eighth wonder of the world. However, despite its grand opening and initial success, the casino faced financial struggles and eventually filed for bankruptcy in 1991, just a year after its launch. This episode in Trump's career highlighted both his tendency to aim for monumental achievements and the risks inherent in his business approach. The Trump Taj Mahal's financial woes were a prelude to several other business challenges, yet Trump's ability to rebound from setbacks became a recurring theme in his narrative.

"Look at my African American over here."

June 3, 2016 (Campaign rally).

Audience: Rally attendees.
Context: Trump pointed out a supporter in the crowd, but his choice of words was criticized for seeming to highlight the individual based solely on race.

Appearance in "Zoolander": Trump made a cameo appearance in the 2001 comedy film "Zoolander." He played himself in a scene where the main character, played by Ben Stiller, competes in a runway walk-off.

"We're going to have insurance for everybody."

January 15, 2017

Audience: General public.

Context: Discussing his plans to replace Obamacare, during a Washington Post interview, Trump promised a healthcare overhaul that would provide coverage for all Americans, a goal that faced challenges in implementation.

The Scottish Golf Course Controversy

Trump's venture into developing a luxury golf course in Aberdeenshire, Scotland, sparked controversy due to environmental concerns and conflicts with local residents. The project, initiated in 2006, involved building a state-of-the-art golf course on a site of special scientific interest, which angered environmentalists and some locals. Trump's dealings in Scotland, including his promises of economic revitalization and clashes with those who opposed his plans, were a prelude to the combative and unyielding style he would later bring to politics. The development of the golf course, and the subsequent documentary "You've Been Trumped" that chronicled the confrontation, underscored Trump's willingness to pursue his vision despite local and environmental opposition.

"I'm the least racist person there is anywhere in the world."

July 30, 2019

Audience: Numerous reporters at a press gaggle.

Context: Responding to accusations of racism, Trump often defended himself with this or similar statements, despite controversy over some of his policies and remarks.

Unsuccessful Airline Venture: In 1989, Trump purchased the Eastern Air Shuttle, a short-haul airline that operated flights between Boston, New York City, and Washington, D.C. He re-branded it as the Trump Shuttle but eventually sold it in 1992 after it accumulated substantial debt.

"People are flushing toilets 10 times, 15 times, as opposed to once."

December 6, 2019

Audience: Business leaders and government officials.
Context: During a White House Round Table on Small Business and Red Tape Reduction Accomplishments, Trump commented on water regulations, suggesting that efficiency standards were too restrictive, leading to this unusual claim.

The Wrestle Mania Appearance

Donald Trump's involvement in the world of professional wrestling, particularly his appearances in WWE events, showcases a unique blend of entertainment and politics. At Wrestle Mania 23 in 2007, Trump participated in the "Battle of the Billionaires" story line, which culminated in a hair vs. hair match with WWE owner Vince McMahon. Each billionaire chose a wrestler to represent them, and the loser's representative would have his head shaved. Trump's wrestler won, leading to the memorable scene of Trump helping to shave Vince McMahon's head in the middle of the ring. This crossover into entertainment underscored Trump's flair for showmanship, a characteristic that would become a hallmark of his political rallies.

"To be blunt, people would vote for me. They just would. Why? Maybe because I'm so good looking."

Various forms over time.

Audience: Various, including media interviews and public appearances.

Context: Trump's comments on his appeal to voters often included a mix of humour and boastfulness, reflecting his confidence in his personal brand and charisma.

Ownership of a Football Team: In addition to his involvement in the USFL, Trump briefly owned the New Jersey Generals football team. He purchased the team in 1983 but sold it before the USFL's final season in 1986.

"It's freezing and snowing in New York – we need global warming!"

November 7, 2012

Audience: Twitter followers.

Context: This tweet showcased Trump's scepticism towards climate change, using a cold weather event to humorously question global warming, despite the scientific consensus on climate change being unaffected by short-term weather variations.

The Art of the Deal and Literary Success

Donald Trump's rise to fame as a businessman was significantly bolstered by the publication of "The Art of the Deal" in 1987. Co-written with journalist Tony Schwartz, the book provides a part memoir, part business advice narrative that cemented Trump's image as a savvy deal maker. It spent 51 weeks on The New York Times Best Seller list, and Trump has often cited it as one of his proudest achievements. The success of "The Art of the Deal" not only elevated Trump's status in the business world but also introduced him to a broader audience as an emblem of success, setting the stage for his eventual foray into reality TV and politics.

"Make America Great Again."

2016 presidential campaign

Audience: American voters.

Context: This slogan became synonymous with Trump's campaign for the presidency, encapsulating his message of restoring the United States' former glory and economic prosperity.

Patented Hairstyle: Trump's distinctive hairstyle has become iconic. In 2011, he received a design patent for the hairstyle from the United States Patent and Trademark Office. The patent describes the arrangement of hair as a "method for styling hair" involving "a side hair portion, a back hair portion, and a top hair portion."

The Mysterious White House Sinkhole

In May 2018, a sinkhole appeared on the White House lawn, sparking a flurry of social media speculation and jokes. This peculiar event occurred near the White House's North Lawn, and it quickly became a metaphor for various political commentary. Trump's response, or lack thereof, to the sinkhole became a humorous anecdote among his critics and supporters alike. While sinkholes in the D.C. area are not uncommon due to the region's geography, the timing and location of this particular sinkhole led to a wide range of interpretations and highlighted how, in the Trump era, even natural occurrences could become politically charged and serve as fodder for the 24-hour news cycle.

"The media is fake."

Date: Frequently used

Audience: General public, rallies, and social media.
Context: Trump often criticized the press for what he perceived as unfair coverage of his administration, contributing to a contentious relationship with many media outlets.

Starred in a Pizza Hut Commercial: Before his foray into politics, Trump appeared in a commercial for Pizza Hut in 1995. The ad featured him enjoying a New York-style pizza while promoting a limited-time offer.

"Nobody respects women more than I do."

October 19, 2016.

Audience: Viewers of the third presidential debate.
Context: Amid various accusations and the release of the "Access Hollywood" tape, Trump sought to counter claims of misogyny by asserting his respect for women.

The Fast Food Banquet

In January 2019, during a government shutdown, Trump hosted the Clemson University football team at the White House to celebrate their national championship. Due to the shutdown, many staff were laid off, so Trump decided to serve a vast array of fast food, claiming it was paid for out of his own pocket. The image of the President proudly presenting a table laden with fast food to elite athletes in the opulent setting of the White House State Dining Room went viral. Critics panned it as un-presidential, while supporters saw it as a relatable, down-to-earth gesture. This event highlighted Trump's penchant for breaking norms and his ability to generate headlines and social media buzz from even the most ordinary actions.

"I will be the greatest jobs president that God ever created."

June 16, 2015.

Audience: Audience at his presidential campaign announcement.
Context: Trump promised significant job creation and economic growth under his administration, emphasizing his business background as a foundation for his capabilities.

TV Ratings Impact: Trump's appearances on television often led to significant spikes in ratings. Whether it was as a guest on talk shows or as the host of "The Apprentice," his presence drew considerable attention from audiences.

"I know more about ISIS than the generals do. Believe me."

November 12, 2015.

Audience: Supporters at a rally in Iowa.
Context: Trump expressed his confidence in his understanding of military matters and terrorism, often critiquing the expertise of established military leaders.

The Historic North Korea Summit

In June 2018, Trump made history by meeting with North Korean leader Kim Jong-un in Singapore, marking the first-ever meeting between a sitting U.S. President and a North Korean leader. This event was part of Trump's unconventional approach to diplomacy, aiming to reduce nuclear tensions and improve relations between the two historically adversarial nations. While the summit and subsequent meetings did not lead to significant denuclearization, they were symbolic of Trump's preference for direct engagement and personal diplomacy, often bypassing traditional diplomatic protocols and processes.

"The concept of shaking hands is absolutely terrible, and statistically I've been proven right."

Date: Various (incl pre-COVID-19).

Audience: Various interviews and discussions.
Context: Known for his germaphobic tendencies, Trump has long criticized handshaking, a stance that gained new relevance during the global health crisis.

Frequent Golfing: During his presidency, Trump was known for his frequent visits to golf courses. He spent a significant amount of time at his own golf resorts, leading to criticism about his work ethic and priorities.

"I think I am, actually humble. I think I'm much more humble than you would understand."

July 17, 2016.

Audience: Interview on "60 Minutes."
Context: Trump's assertion of humility, presented in his characteristic bragging manner, was part of a discussion on his personality and leadership style.

Purchasing Greenland

In 2019, reports surfaced that Trump had expressed interest in purchasing Greenland from Denmark, a proposal that was quickly dismissed by Danish officials. The idea, reminiscent of the United States' purchase of Alaska, was met with a mix of amusement and bewilderment. Trump's proposal brought unexpected attention to Greenland and sparked discussions about the strategic value of territories in the modern world. It also illustrated Trump's unconventional approach to geopolitics, viewing it through a business lens.

"Windmills are the greatest threat in the US to both bald and golden eagles. Media claims fictional 'global warming' is worse."

September 9, 2014.

Audience: Twitter followers.
Context: Demonstrating his scepticism of renewable energy sources and climate change, Trump's tweet reflected his controversial stance on environmental issues.

Trademark Applications: Trump and his businesses have filed for trademarks on a wide range of products and services in countries around the world, including Trump-branded clothing, hotels, and even "Trump Steaks."

"I have a natural instinct for science."

October 17, 2018.

Audience: Interview with the Associated Press.
Context: Despite a lack of formal scientific training, Trump

asserted his innate understanding of science, particularly in discussions around climate change and environmental policy.

Feeding Koi Fish with Shinzo Abe

During a visit to Japan in 2017, Trump and Japanese Prime Minister Shinzo Abe participated in the traditional feeding of koi fish. A video clip showed Trump apparently growing impatient and dumping his entire box of fish food into the pond, a moment that quickly went viral. Critics used it to suggest Trump's lack of diplomacy and patience. However, fuller video footage showed Abe doing the same under more controlled circumstances.

"We're going to build a wall, and Mexico is going to pay for it."
Date: Throughout his 2016 campaign.

Audience: Supporters at campaign rallies.

Context: One of Trump's most famous campaign promises, this quote symbolized his tough stance on immigration and border security. The financing and construction of the wall became a central and contentious policy debate.

Multiple Marriages: Trump has been married three times. His first two marriages, to Ivanka Trump and Marla Maples, ended in divorce. He is currently married to Melania Trump, a former Slovenian model, whom he wed in 2005.

Buying Silence on UFOs

Trump once joked in an interview that he could take drastic measures to ensure former President Barack Obama remained silent about UFOs, saying, "I know nothing about it, but it's very interesting. I could certainly send him to Guantanamo. I'm sure he knows something."

This tongue-in-cheek remark highlighted Trump's flair for dramatic statements and his willingness to engage with conspiracy theories, as well as his unique sense of humour when discussing sensitive topics.

"The American dream is dead."

June 16, 2015.

Audience: Presidential campaign announcement speech.
Context: Trump's assertion that the American dream was defunct fuelled his campaign narrative of economic decline and the need for a political outsider to rejuvenate the nation.

Education Donation Controversy: There was controversy surrounding the Trump Foundation, a charitable organization established by Trump and his family. It faced allegations of self-dealing and was ordered to dissolve in 2019 after admitting to improper use of funds.

"You're fired!"

Date: "The Apprentice," 2004 to 2017.

Audience: Contestants on the show and viewers.
Context: Trump's catchphrase became widely associated with his persona as a tough, no-nonsense business leader, furthering his public image.

The Secret Service and COVID-19

Amid the COVID-19 pandemic, Trump's insistence on maintaining a public schedule raised concerns for the health and safety of the Secret

Service agents tasked with his protection. Notably, during a hospital stay for COVID-19 treatment, Trump took a short drive to wave to supporters outside, an act that necessitated the presence of Secret Service agents in the enclosed space of the vehicle. This decision was criticized for potentially exposing the agents to the virus, highlighting the challenges and controversies of presidential security in the context of a global pandemic.

"It's going to be huge!"

Date: Various occasions.

Audience: Various, including campaign rallies and media interviews.

Context: Trump's use of "huge" to describe his plans and ambitions became a signature phrase, reflecting his penchant for grandiosity and frequent exaggeration.

Trump Vodka: In 2006, Trump launched Trump Vodka, hoping to capitalize on his brand's association with luxury and success. However, the brand was discontinued in 2011 due to lacklustre sales.

"I think I have a great temperament."

September 26, 2016.

Audience: First presidential debate against Hillary Clinton.

Context: Trump defended his temperament in the face of criticism, countering claims that he lacked the temperament necessary for the presidency.

The Diet Coke Button

One of the more light-hearted revelations about Trump's time in the Oval Office was the existence of a so-called "Diet Coke button." With a press of this button, situated on the Resolute Desk, Trump could summon a butler to bring him a Diet Coke. The button became a symbol of the peculiarities and personal quirks of the presidency, showing how the holders of the office could tailor it to their personal preferences, no matter how small.

"Nobody has better respect for women than I do. Nobody."

Date: Various occasions.

Audience: Various, including campaign events and interviews.
Context: Trump frequently made assertions about his respect for women, despite facing numerous accusations of misogyny and inappropriate behaviour towards women.

Fast Food Aficionado: Trump has publicly expressed a fondness for fast food, particularly McDonald's and KFC. He has been photographed eating fast food on numerous occasions, even serving it to guests at the White House during official visits.

"I have made the tough decisions, always with an eye toward the bottom line."

Date: Various occasions.

Audience: Various, including interviews and business-related events.

Context: Trump often highlighted his track record of making decisive choices in his business ventures, framing himself as a decisive leader focused on financial success.

The "Big, Beautiful Wall"

Trump's promise to build a "big, beautiful wall" along the U.S.-Mexico border was a central theme of both his campaigns and presidency. The wall, intended to curb illegal immigration, became a symbol of his administration's hardline immigration policies. Despite the logistical, legal, and financial challenges, small portions of the wall were constructed. The wall remains a divisive symbol, representing for some a necessary measure for national security, and for others, a symbol of America's isolationism and xenophobia.

"I alone can fix it."

Date: July 21, 2016.

Audience: Republican National Convention.

Context: Trump emphasized his confidence in his ability to solve the nation's problems, presenting himself as a strong leader during his acceptance speech as the Republican nominee for president.

Critique of Wind Energy: Trump has been vocal in his criticism of wind energy, often referring to wind turbines as "ugly" and claiming they are harmful to birds. He has fought against wind farm projects near his golf courses in Scotland.

"The American Dream is back. We're going to create an environment for small business like we haven't had in many, many decades!"

December 22, 2017.

Audience: Twitter followers.

Context: Trump tweeted this message in an attempt to highlight his administration's focus on revitalizing small businesses and fostering economic growth.

Failed Bid for the Time Warner Building: In 1994, Trump attempted to purchase the iconic Time Warner Building in New York City. Despite his efforts, the bid fell through, and the building was eventually sold to a different buyer.

The Sharpie Hurricane Map

In 2019, Trump displayed a hurricane forecast map that appeared to have been altered with a Sharpie to include Alabama in the path of Hurricane Dorian, contrary to official forecasts. The incident, widely known as "Sharpiegate," led to discussions about the integrity of official communications and the politicization of weather forecasting. It exemplified the lengths to which Trump would go to defend his statements, even in the face of contradictory evidence.

"You have to think anyway, so why not think big?"

Date: published in 2004.

Audience: Readers.
Context: Trump advocated for ambitious thinking and bold aspirations as keys to success in business and life.

The Miss Universe Mishap

Before his presidency, Trump co-owned the Miss Universe Organization. In 2015, during the Miss Universe pageant finale, a significant blunder occurred when host Steve Harvey mistakenly announced Miss Colombia as the winner, only to correct himself minutes later, declaring Miss Philippines the true victor. Trump, who had sold his ownership stake earlier that year, took to social media to comment on the mix-up, suggesting that such a mistake would not have happened under his watch. This incident underscored Trump's continued interest and influence in the world of entertainment and beauty pageants, even as he shifted his focus to politics.

"It's a very scary time for young men in America when you can be guilty of something that you may not be guilty of."

Date: October 2, 2018.

Audience: Reporters.
Context: Trump made this remark while discussing allegations

of sexual misconduct against then-Supreme Court nominee Brett Kavanaugh, expressing concern about the impact on men accused of such offences.

Ran for President in 2000: Trump explored a presidential run in 2000, seeking the nomination of the Reform Party. Although he eventually dropped out of the race, he made several campaign stops and participated in debates.

"When somebody challenges you, fight back. Be brutal, be tough."

Date: published in 2004.

Audience: Readers.
Context: Trump advocated for assertiveness and resilience in the face of challenges, promoting a combative approach to competition and adversity.

The Space Force Creation

One of Trump's most futuristic initiatives was the establishment of the United States Space Force as the sixth branch of the U.S. Armed Forces in December 2019. This decision marked the first new military service since the Air Force was created in 1947. Trump touted the Space Force as a necessary step to ensure America's dominance in space, citing potential threats from other nations. The creation of the Space Force was met with mixed reactions, from those who criticized it as unnecessary to others who applauded it as a visionary move. Regardless, it underscored Trump's willingness to pursue ambitious and often controversial initiatives.

"I've been treated very unfairly by this judge. Now, this judge is of Mexican heritage. I'm building a wall, okay? I'm building a wall."

Date: June 3, 2016.

Audience: Rally in San Diego, California.
Context: Trump criticised Judge Gonzalo Curiel's handling of a lawsuit against Trump University, suggesting bias due to the judge's ethnicity, which sparked controversy and accusations of racism.

Extensive Litigations: Over the years, Trump and his businesses have been involved in thousands of legal actions. He has utilised litigation as a business strategy and faced numerous lawsuits ranging from contract disputes to defamation cases.

"I don't think Ivanka would do that [pose for Playboy], although she does have a very nice figure. I've said if Ivanka weren't my daughter, perhaps I'd be dating her."

Date: Various occasions.

Audience: Various interviews, including "The Howard Stern Show."
Context: Trump's comments about his daughter Ivanka received widespread criticism for their inappropriate nature, even though they were made in a joking manner.

The G7 Summit Proposal for Doral

Trump faced criticism for suggesting his Doral golf resort in Miami as the venue for the 2020 G7 summit, a move that raised concerns about potential conflicts of interest and the use of presidential power for personal gain. Although he later retracted the suggestion, the incident highlighted ongoing concerns about the intersection of his business dealings and his role as President, sparking debates about the emoluments clause of the U.S. Constitution.

"They're not coming from Norway, let's put it that way."

Date: January 11, 2018.

Audience: Meeting on immigration reform.

Context: Trump made this remark during a discussion on immigration, contrasting immigrants from Norway with those from Haiti, El Salvador, and African countries, sparking accusations of racism.

Impeachment Records: Donald Trump is the first U.S. president in history to be impeached twice by the House of Representatives – first in December 2019 and then again in January 2021. However, he was acquitted by the Senate on both occasions.

"We have to get our youth back to respecting authority and respecting law enforcement."

Date: August 22, 2017.

Audience: Speech at a rally in Phoenix, Arizona.

Context: Trump spoke about restoring law and order, advocating for increased respect for authority figures and law enforcement agencies, a central theme of his presidency.

"I think I've made a lot of sacrifices. I work very, very hard."

Date: July 30, 2016.

Audience: Interview with ABC News.

Context: Trump responded to criticism from the parents of a fallen soldier, suggesting that his business success constituted significant personal sacrifices.

The St. Patrick's Day Shamrock Bowl Incident

In a light-hearted diplomatic gaffe, Trump once praised Irish immigrants for their contributions to the USA during a St. Patrick's Day event but mistakenly read a quote from his prepared speech that he attributed to an Irish proverb. It later emerged that the quote was not Irish at all but rather a poem by Nigerian poet Albashir Adam Alhassan. The mix-up was a humorous reminder of the pitfalls of not thoroughly vetting speech materials.

"I'm speaking with myself, number one, because I have a very good brain and I've said a lot of things."

Date: March 16, 2016.

Audience: Interview on MSNBC's "Morning Joe."

Context: Trump discussed his approach to foreign policy, suggesting that he relied on his own judgement and intellect in decision-making processes.

Real Estate Legacy: Trump's mark on the New York City skyline is significant, with Trump Tower on Fifth Avenue being one of his most famous real estate developments. The building serves as his main residence and the headquarters of The Trump Organization.

"Sometimes by losing a battle you find a new way to win the war."

Date: "The Art of the Deal" published in 1987.

Audience: Readers.
Context: Trump's reflection on strategy emphasized the importance of adaptability and resilience in achieving long-term success.

The Eclipse Viewing Revisited

Despite the widespread attention the first incident received, Trump had another notable moment with a solar eclipse. In a subsequent viewing, equipped with proper safety glasses this time, he humorously revisited the previous mishap by initially glancing at the sky before donning the glasses. This playful acknowledgment of his earlier mistake was a rare moment of self-deprecation, showing a lighter side to his often combative public persona.

"I'm the Ernest Hemingway of 140 characters."

Date: December 6, 2016.

Audience: Twitter followers.
Context: Trump compared his succinct and impactful tweets

to the concise writing style of the renowned author Ernest Hemingway, highlighting his ability to convey messages effectively on social media.

Business Before Politics: Before entering politics, Donald Trump was well-known as a real estate mogul and a television personality, particularly for his role on "The Apprentice" where his catchphrase "You're fired!" became widely recognized.

"I think I'll win the Hispanic vote."

Date: June 16, 2015.

Audience: Interview on NBC's "Meet the Press."

Context: Trump expressed confidence in his ability to secure support from Hispanic voters, despite controversial remarks about immigration that had drawn criticism from the Latino community.

Offer to Buy a Golf Course in Ireland

Reflecting his business background and love for golf, Trump once made an unsolicited offer to buy a golf course in Ireland because he thought it had great potential. The owner, not interested in selling, was surprised by the directness of the approach. This anecdote showcases Trump's spontaneous business instincts and how they occasionally surfaced in unexpected ways during his presidency and personal dealings.

"You're not gonna raise that f**kin' price, you understand me?"

Date: From "The Art of the Deal" published in 1987.

Audience: Business negotiations.
Context: This quote illustrates Trump's aggressive negotiation style and willingness to assert control in business dealings.

Golf Course Magnate: Beyond skyscrapers, Trump has a substantial footprint in the world of golf, owning several luxury golf resorts around the world, including the famous Trump National Golf Club in Bedminster, New Jersey.

"I'm very highly educated. I know words; I have the best words."

Date: December 30, 2015.

Audience: Campaign rally in Hilton Head, South Carolina.
Context: Trump boasted about his intelligence and communication skills.

Two Corinthians

During the 2016 campaign, Trump's attempt to connect with Christian evangelical voters led to an amusing gaffe when he referred to the Second Epistle to the Corinthians in the Bible as "Two Corinthians" during a speech at Liberty University. The mistake was quickly seized upon by media and critics as evidence of his unfamiliarity with the Bible, despite his strong evangelical support. This incident underscored the cultural and sometimes comical misunderstandings that could arise from Trump's direct appeal to diverse voter groups.

"The point is, you can never be too greedy."

Date: "How to Get Rich," published in 2004.

Audience: Readers.

Context: Trump's assertion about the pursuit of wealth underscores his belief in the importance of ambition and financial success.

Healthcare Legislation Attempt: During his presidency, Trump made a significant attempt to repeal and replace the Affordable Healthcare Care Act (Obamacare), a hallmark policy of his predecessor, Barack Obama. Although the repeal efforts passed in the House of Representatives, they failed in the Senate.

"I have great respect for the UK. United Kingdom. Great respect. People call it Britain. They call it Great Britain. They used to call it England, different parts."

Date: January 16, 2017.

Audience: Interview with Michael Gove for The Times of London.

Context: Trump's statement, while well-intentioned, demonstrated a lack of understanding of the UK's political and geographic distinctions, leading to some confusion and amusement Delete this text prior to use.

Made in the USA
Monee, IL
01 December 2025

36972964R00026